VOLUME TWO

the Best of the Great Songwriters

Production: Sadie Cook and Carole Staff

Published 1995

© International Music Publications Limited
Southend Road, Woodford Green, Essex IG8 8HN, England

VOLUME TWO

the Best of the Great Songwriters

A COUPLE OF SWELLS

Words and Music by
IRVING BERLIN

5

REFRAIN

ALFIE

Words by HAL DAVID
Music by BURT BACHARACH

FORTY SECOND STREET

Words by AL DUBIN
Music by HARRY WARREN

HAPPY TALK

Words by OSCAR HAMMERSTEIN II
Music by RICHARD RODGERS

15

16

IV Refrain

HOW DO YOU KEEP THE MUSIC PLAYING?

Words by ALAN BERGMAN
and MARILYN BERGMAN
Music by MICHEL LEGRAND

LET'S CALL THE WHOLE THING OFF

Music and Lyrics by
GEORGE GERSHWIN and IRA GERSHWIN

REFRAIN

I GET A KICK OUT OF YOU

Words and Music by
COLE PORTER

29

I ONLY HAVE EYES FOR YOU

Words by AL DUBIN
Music by HARRY WARREN

*Diagrams for Guitar, Symbols for Ukulele and Banjo

IT HAD TO BE YOU

Words by GUS KAHN
Music by ISHAM JONES

Why do I do just as you say,___ why must I just give you your way.___
Seems like dreams like I al-ways had,___ could be, should be mak-ing me glad.___

Why do I sigh,___ why don't I try_to for - get? It must have
Why am I blue?___ it's up to you_to ex - plain. I'm think-ing

37

38

LOSING MY MIND

Words and Music by
STEPHEN SONDHEIM

41

MAGIC MOMENTS

Words by HAL DAVID
Music by BURT BACHARACH

44

LOVE IS HERE TO STAY

Music and Lyrics by
GEORGE GERSHWIN and IRA GERSHWIN

The more I read the pa-pers The less I com-pre-hend The

world and all its ca-pers And how it all will end. Noth-ing seems to be

47

MAD DOGS AND ENGLISHMEN

Words and Music by
NOEL COWARD

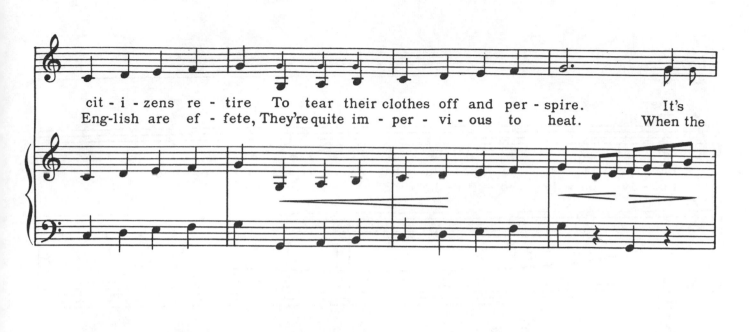

cit - i - zens re - tire To tear their clothes off and per - spire. It's
Eng-lish are ef - fete, They're quite im - per - vi - ous to heat. When the

one of those rules that the great-est fools o - bey, _____ Be-cause the
white man rides ev - 'ry na - tive hides in glee. _____ Be-cause the

Cm   Bb   Ab   G   E7   B7

sun is much too sul-try And one must a-void its ul-try-vio-let
sim-ple crea-tures hope he Will im - pale his so - lar to-pee on a

E   B7   E   G7

52

REFRAIN

MAKIN' WHOOPEE!

Words by GUS KAHN
Music by WALTER DONALDSON

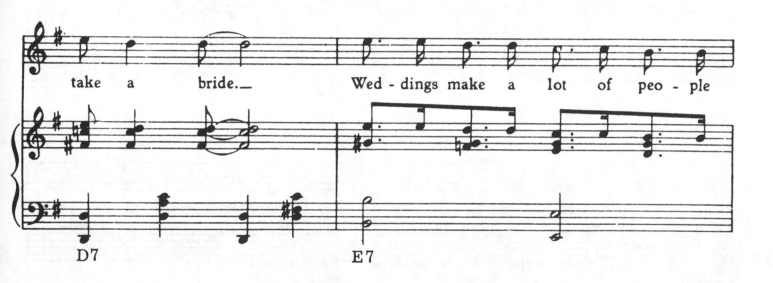

58

REFRAIN

MY BABY JUST CARES FOR ME

Words by GUS KAHN
Music by WALTER DONALDSON

62

SEND IN THE CLOWNS

Words and Music by
STEPHEN SONDHEIM

MY FUNNY VALENTINE

Words by LORENZ HART
Music by RICHARD RODGERS

Moderato

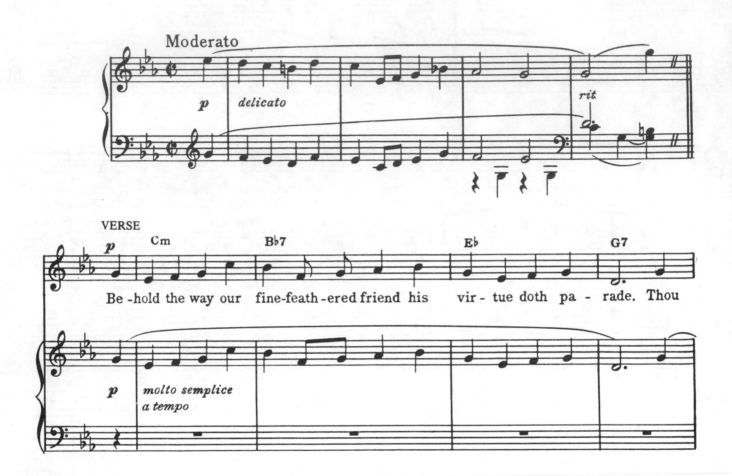

VERSE

Be -hold the way our fine-feath -ered friend his vir - tue doth pa - rade. Thou

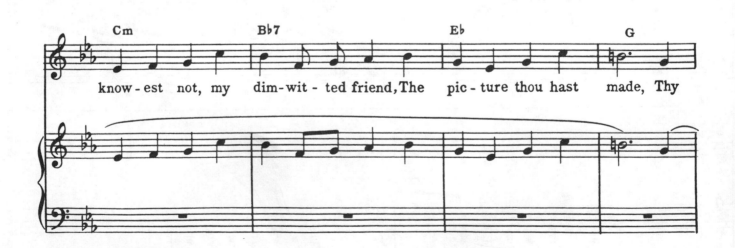

know-est not, my dim-wit - ted friend, The pic - ture thou hast made, Thy

THE NEARNESS OF YOU

Words by NED WASHINGTON
Music by HOAGY CARMICHAEL

NIGHT AND DAY

Words and Music by
COLE PORTER

74

SKYLARK

Words by JOHNNY MERCER
Music by HOAGY CARMICHAEL

78

SOME ENCHANTED EVENING

Words by OSCAR HAMMERSTEIN II
Music by RICHARD RODGERS

80

SOMEONE TO WATCH OVER ME

Music and Lyrics by
GEORGE GERSHWIN and IRA GERSHWIN

87

TRUE LOVE

Words and Music by
COLE PORTER

WHAT ARE YOU DOING FOR THE REST OF YOUR LIFE?

Words by ALAN BERGMAN
and MARILYN BERGMAN
Music by MICHEL LEGRAND

WHAT'LL I DO?

Words and Music b
IRVING BERLI

97

WITH A SONG IN MY HEART

Words by LORENZ HART
Music by RICHARD RODGERS

VERSE

YOU'LL NEVER KNOW

Words by MACK GORDON
Music by HARRY WARREN

YOUNGER THAN SPRINGTIME

Words by OSCAR HAMMERSTEIN II
Music by RICHARD RODGERS

105

107

5/97

Printed by
Halstan & Co. Ltd., Amersham, Bucks., England